FOR DEREK -

Thanks for your help,
advice and direction

I know we are going to
rock this town!

Run it up!

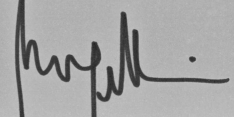

# MOUNT GAY®RUM

# Infusion!

spirited cooking by paul yellin

MACMILLAN
CARIBBEAN

MOUNT GAY®RUM
BARBADOS

Macmillan Education
Between Towns Road, Oxford OX4 3PP
A division of Macmillan Publishers Limited
Companies and representatives throughout the world

www.macmillan-caribbean.com

ISBN 1 4050 1721 X

First published 2003

Text by Paul Yellin
Designed by Sean Michael Field & Alison Forde-Alleyne for
Ikon Design [t] 246-434-4566 [e] ikondesign@caribsurf.com
Cover design by Ikon Design
Cover photograph by Julie Webster

Photography by Julie Webster
Food styling by Paul Yellin and Julie Webster

Printed in China

2007  2006  2005  2004  2003
10  9  8  7  6  5  4  3  2  1

# contents

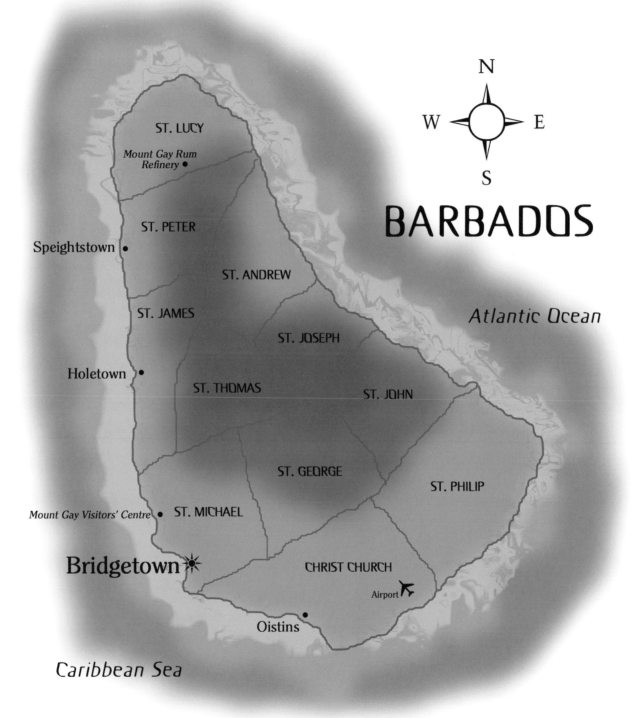

ST. LUCY

Mount Gay Rum
Refinery •

ST. PETER

Speightstown •

ST. ANDREW

ST. JAMES

ST. JOSEPH

Holetown •

ST. THOMAS

ST. JOHN

ST. GEORGE

ST. PHILIP

Mount Gay Visitors' Centre •   ST. MICHAEL

Bridgetown ☀

CHRIST CHURCH

Airport ✈

Oistins •

Caribbean Sea

Atlantic Ocean

N
W · E
S

BARBADOS

# Thank You

To my mum who was mostly supportive despite being the only person I know allergic to rum! My grandparents Anne and Jack who remind me how short life is, and my partner Cindy who makes me smile each day.

## ACKNOWLEDGEMENTS

So many people have made a contribution to this project (some unknowingly) and I would like to warmly thank all of them, with pre-apologies to anyone I forgot. The team of young professionals - Julie, Sean and Alison who put the concept into reality. The Mount Gay Family - Jean-Noel Reynaud - Managing Director, Peter Marshall "The Rum God" - Sales & Marketing Director, Jerry Edwards - Master Blender & Operations Manager, Robyn Gollop-Knight - International Brand Manager, who made this happen!, Claire Jordan - North American Brand Manager, who requested the first rum recipes, Chesterfield Browne & Chris Breedy - top class mixologists!

Honourable mention to the Ward family - keepers of tradition, notably, Louis Ward and Carl Ward for providing invaluable 11th hour advice and assistance. I am proud to know they approve of my ideas and experiments with the rum their family has made for centuries.

The friends and family who provide encouragement, honesty and the environment to be the lunatics we really are - a diverse group of characters each with a talent and plan. My cousins Jason and Jennifer, Adriana who loved Barbados, and Aunt Nancy, not always in touch, but in my thoughts, The Straughns', The Harpers', The Ho family, The Watermans', The Hartmanns', J. Welch - the stories when we are old! M.Waterman - this guy can do anything! G. Markle - work hard, play hard! S. Davis - a good man and friend, N. Donowa - alive all the time! J. Brathwaite - never forget the plan, M. Chandler - a tough year for all, A. McDonald - we almost fought at our first meeting 20 years ago...! C. Rudder - find a way my brother... A. Harper - from day one... K. Gill - if it ain't illegal, it should be! R.Ho - ashamed we don't stay in touch, but I always have time for you. And finally, to all the chefs, kitchen & restaurant staff from whom I learned over the years.

**SWEET ENDINGS -** Richard White, Mellow Stuff Bakery. All desserts were designed and made with Richard who is as honest as he is talented.

Special thanks to the companies that donated most of the food used in these recipes. Top quality and freshness are the cornerstone of these successful businesses and meals...

## HOTEL FOOD SUPPLIES
Tony Pickering, Mrs Adams, Paulette Sobers, Kenny Hewitt

## SHORELINZ SEAFOOD SPECIALISTS
Richard Sumpter, Christian Black, Jasper Seymour

## PLATEWARE, GLASSWARE AND PROPS
Maggie Bell - **Red Clay Potteries** - Fairfield, St Michael
Wendy Tatum - **Details** - Holetown, St James
Sue Yellin - **My Blue Heaven** - Brighton, St Michael
David Spieler - **Earthworks** - Edgehill, St Thomas

# History of Mount Gay Rum

## 300 Years

The story of Mount Gay Rum began in the Caribbean island of Barbados, a coral island measuring only 14 miles wide by 21 miles long.

Sugar is harvested and boiled to produce a thick dark treacle-like substance called molasses. This rich molasses together with the island's unique supply of pure underground spring water, make the base for a flavourful beverage. Although sugar cane was being grown in many other parts of the world during the 1600s, Barbados is widely accepted as the birth-place of rum.

Many people believe that rum was being produced on the Mount Gay Rum Estate from as early as 1663. However, the first surviving written evidence of this is a legal deed dated 20th February 1703; this deed lists the property and the equipment found on the Estate, including equipment essential for the manufacture of rum.

As such, Mount Gay Rum is one of the world's oldest and finest rums, and 300 years of its remarkable story was celebrated in February 2003.

# History of Mount Gay Rum
## 300 Years

The Mount Gay Rum Estate, which lies on a ridge in St Lucy (the northernmost parish of Barbados), was originally known as Mount Gilboa. In 1801 it was renamed Mount Gay to honour the late estate caretaker and eminent son of Barbados, Sir John Gay Alleyne.

In the early 1900s, Aubrey Ward, a prominent Barbadian businessman, bought the estate. He introduced new methods to meet the increasing demand for Mount Gay Rum, while strictly maintaining its traditional character. Along with his business partner and marketing specialist John Hutson, he introduced Mount Gay Rum to the world market. Mr Ward's son Mr Darnley DaCosta Ward continued these efforts until he passed away in 1989.

*Aubrey Ward*

The Ward family continues to be involved with Mount Gay Rum Distilleries, majority interest of which was acquired by the Remy Cointreau Group in 1989. That move has taken the company in a new direction, allowing it to benefit from the French multinational's extensive distribution network and international marketing acumen.

*The Master Blender test tasting*

# History of Mount Gay Rum

The process by which Mount Gay Rums are created starts with lush, green fields of high quality sugar cane. The sugar cane plant takes 12-18 months to mature. It is harvested between the months of February and June when the sugar content within the plant reaches its peak. The harvested cane is then taken to the sugar refinery.

Juice is squeezed from the cane fibres and heated to produce sugar crystals. The residue left over from the boiling process is a thick black syrup known as molasses. The molasses is mixed with pure Barbados water in huge oak vats, and slowly the sugars are converted to alcohol. This is the first stage in the production of this delicious spirit.

One of the unique features in the making of Mount Gay Rum is the use of two different distillation methods, yielding alcohols that are distinct in character.

Single distilled alcohol is produced by a process of continuous fractional distillation in a Coffey Still. This distillate is 97% alcohol by volume and possesses a subtle rum character.

# History <u>of Mount Gay Rum</u>

## rum process

The second method is that of batch distillation through traditional pot stills. These have been in use since the 1700s. Distillation is accomplished batch by batch in centuries-old copper stills. The double distillate or pot-stilled rum is of a lower alcohol strength (about 86%), but it has a more intense and robust character than the single distillate. When well matured, it acquires a superb, intensely aromatic character. Herein lies one of the keys to the exceptional taste of Mount Gay Rum, the unique flavourful character imparted by our own centuries-old Copper Pot Still.

The two types of distillates are stored for several years in only the finest quality white-oak barrels. These barrels are slightly charred to impart a distinctive smoky flavour and rich colour to the spirit - another unique feature of Mount Gay Rum.

Once matured, the single and double distillates are expertly 'married' by our Master Blender to produce the various products in the Mount Gay Rum range. Superb blending is a feature of all Mount Gay Rums, and is a key differentiating factor that sets Mount Gay Rum apart from its competitors.

# History of Mount Gay Rum

## rum process

From its humble beginnings, this fine spirit has grown to be one of the favourites of rum lovers around the world. Today Mount Gay Eclipse Rum, the brand flagship, and Mount Gay Extra Old Rum are available in over 60 countries and have amassed several awards for excellence. And, with an unflinching dedication to the production of quality spirits, Mount Gay Rum continues to emerge as the discerning consumers' rum of choice.

The launch of Mount Gay Rum *Infusion, Spirited Cooking* by Paul Yellin is one of the many initiatives undertaken to commemorate the first 300 years of Mount Gay Rum. It is hoped that Paul's collection of imaginative recipes and the selection of Chester's famous cocktails will encourage you to experiment with the products in the Mount Gay Rum range and savour our quality spirit in new and exciting ways.

# How to Use This Book

*Let's assume the reader has basic culinary skills and comprehension, so detailed explanation is not necessary. I suggest to all people who like food and cooking, to get a copy of the Food Lover's Companion (Sharon Tyler Herbst) Barron's Cooking Guide. It is a dictionary/glossary of all things & terms culinary.*

*The recipes are comfortable approximations and true yield may vary depending on actual size of produce. The dishes should serve 4-6, depending on appetite. The cocktail recipes give ingredients for 1 glass of the cocktail.*

*Rum and spiciness (pepper) are used freely in these pages. All amounts are suggestions and can be adjusted for pleasure or pain.*

*Always use less and add to taste...you cannot take it out once it's in.*

*Read recipes first and organize ingredients and equipment needed to prepare up to point of cooking, then follow the method.*

Alcohol and food have a very important role in our social and cultural structure, not only in Barbados, but all over the world... Memories are made and rekindled with smells and tastes and hopefully allow you to recapture a little bit of that time. After a few years working in large kitchens 6-7 nights a week, with literally thousands of meals prepared, I can state that cooking is an art, and not an exact science, so here are a few tips to help....

*With repetition comes skill and technique.*
*It takes time and each recipe will adjust and*
*adapt to the cook's own style.*

*There will always be some adjustments for taste,*
*simply because produce isn't always consistent...*
*Suppliers, restaurants, markets and grocers all*
*shop competitively for the best price vs. availability,*
*so they may not always get the same product.*

*Simplicity is key in combining flavours and*
*presenting food. Natural colours attract the eye*
*and represent the tastes.*

*Cooking, I find, is an extension of personality and*
*more importantly, at the time of cooking your*
*moods are projected through. When cooking with*
*rum, try to be in an upbeat, fun, tropical mood*
*and share the experience with loved ones.*

*When preparing any of these recipes, feel free*
*to pour yourself a glass, or mix a cocktail from*
*our award winning selection, to help create the*
*mood and spirit Mount Gay Rum represents.*

*Enjoy!*

Warning!
Rum will ignite when exposed to an open flame!
Please take into account personal safety and common
sense while pouring in to some dishes.
When you learn how, it can be impressive and look great!
Be careful.

# equivalents & temperatures

# Table of Equivalents

The exact equivalents in the following tables have been rounded for convenience.

*US/UK*

| | |
|---|---|
| *oz=ounce* | *g=gram* |
| *lb=pound* | *kg=kilogram* |
| *in=inch* | *mm=millimetre* |
| *ft=foot* | *cm=centimetre* |
| *tsp=teaspoon* | *ml=millilitre* |
| *tbsp=tablespoon* | *l=litre* |
| *fl oz=fluid ounce* | |
| *qt=quart* | |

*METRIC*

*WEIGHTS*

| *US/UK* | *METRIC* |
|---|---|
| *1 oz* | *30 g* |
| *2 oz* | *60 g* |
| *3 oz* | *90 g* |
| *4 oz (1/4 lb)* | *125 g* |
| *5 oz (1/3 lb)* | *155 g* |
| *6 oz* | *185 g* |
| *7 oz* | *220 g* |
| *8 oz (1/2 lb)* | *250 g* |
| *10 oz* | *315 g* |
| *12 oz (3/4 lb)* | *375 g* |
| *14 oz* | *440 g* |
| *16 oz (1 lb)* | *500 g* |
| *1 1/2 lb* | *750 g* |
| *2 lb* | *1 kg* |
| *3 lb* | *1.5 kg* |

| FAHRENHEIT | CELSIUS | GAS |
|------------|---------|-----|
| 250 | 120 | 1/2 |
| 275 | 140 | 1 |
| 300 | 150 | 2 |
| 325 | 160 | 3 |
| 350 | 180 | 4 |
| 375 | 190 | 5 |
| 400 | 200 | 6 |
| 425 | 220 | 7 |
| 450 | 230 | 8 |
| 475 | 240 | 9 |
| 500 | 260 | 10 |

LIQUIDS

| US | METRIC | UK |
|----|--------|-----|
| 2 tbsp | 30 ml | 1 fl oz |
| 1/4 cup | 60 ml | 2 fl oz |
| 1/3 cup | 80 ml | 3 fl oz |
| 1/2 cup | 125 ml | 4 fl oz |
| 2/3 cup | 160 ml | 5 fl oz |
| 3/4 cup | 180 ml | 6 fl oz |
| 1 cup | 250 ml | 8 fl oz |
| 11/2 cups | 375 ml | 12 fl oz |
| 2 cups | 500 ml | 16 fl oz |
| 4 cups/1 qt | 1 l | 32 fl oz |

# imbibe
# cocktails

# Passionate Colada

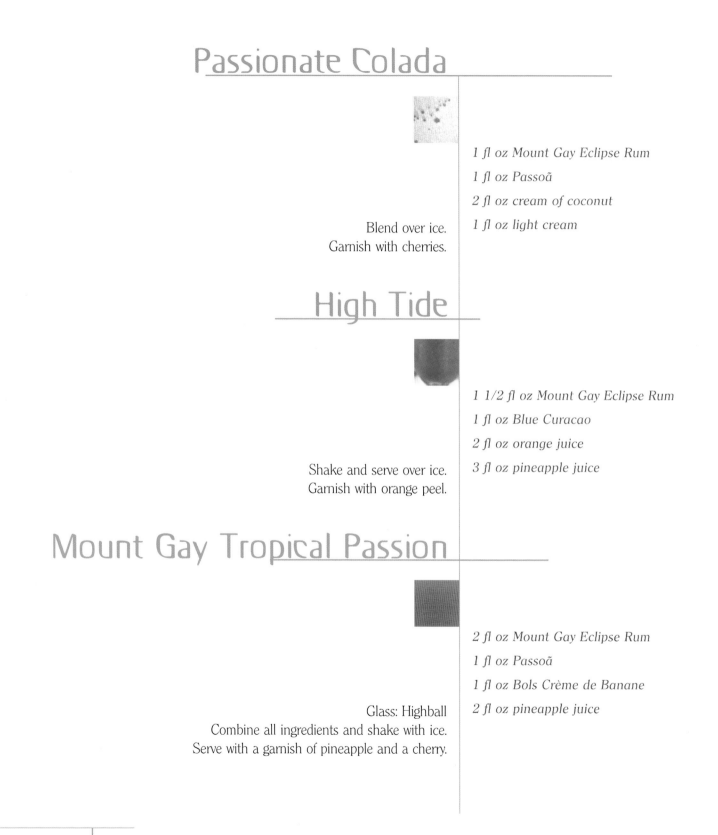

1 fl oz Mount Gay Eclipse Rum

1 fl oz Passoã

2 fl oz cream of coconut

1 fl oz light cream

Blend over ice.
Garnish with cherries.

# High Tide

1 1/2 fl oz Mount Gay Eclipse Rum

1 fl oz Blue Curacao

2 fl oz orange juice

3 fl oz pineapple juice

Shake and serve over ice.
Garnish with orange peel.

# Mount Gay Tropical Passion

2 fl oz Mount Gay Eclipse Rum

1 fl oz Passoã

1 fl oz Bols Crème de Banane

2 fl oz pineapple juice

Glass: Highball
Combine all ingredients and shake with ice.
Serve with a garnish of pineapple and a cherry.

# Melon Dramatic

1 1/2 fl oz Mount Gay Eclipse Rum

1 1/2 fl oz melon liqueur

2 fl oz orange juice

2 fl oz pineapple juice

Shake and serve over ice.
Garnish with a slice of melon.

1 fl oz passion fruit juice

# Mount Gay Rum Punch

3 fl oz Mount Gay Rum Eclipse Rum

2 fl oz lime juice

2 1/2 fl oz simple syrup

1/4 fl oz Angostura bitters

Fill 12 fl oz glass with ice.
Pour rum, lime juice, simple syrup and bitters over ice.
Fill glass with water and sprinkle nutmeg on top.
Garnish with cherry.

1 pinch nutmeg

# Mount Gay Rum Sea Breeze

*1 1/2 fl oz Mount Gay Eclipse Rum*

*3 fl oz grapefruit juice*

Shake and serve over ice.
Garnish with a wedge of orange.

*2 fl oz cranberry juice*

# Sunrise Surprise

*1 1/2 fl oz Mount Gay Eclipse Rum*

*1 fl oz Galliano*

*4 fl oz orange juice*

Mix rum, galliano and juice together with ice.
Pour grenadine over the blend.
Garnish with a cherry and a slice of orange.

*1/2 fl oz grenadine syrup*

# Mount Gay Rum Fizz

1 1/2 fl oz Mount Gay Eclipse Rum

4 fl oz orange juice

3 fl oz soda water

1 oz plain sweetener

Blend with ice.
Garnish with a cherry and a slice of orange.

# Koko Desire

1 1/2 fl oz  Mount Gay Eclipse Rum

1 1/2 fl oz Ponche Kuba

1 1/2 fl oz light cream

2 1/2 fl oz cream of coconut

1 fl oz crème de cacao

Blend with ice.
Garnish with grated nutmeg.

# 300th Anniversary Cocktail

2 fl oz Mount Gay Extra Old Rum

1 fl oz Amaretto

3/4 fl oz crème de banane

4 fl oz pineapple juice

Shake and serve in a high ball glass.
Garnish with pineapple slice and a sprig of mint.

# first
# impressions

# Roasted Pumpkin and Ginger Soup

You Need

4 tbsp butter

1-2 garlic cloves chopped

1 tbsp minced ginger

1/4 cup oil mix (25% pomace, olive oil
and 75% vegetable oil)

3 medium onions chopped

3 medium potatoes chopped

2 cups chopped pumpkin

1/3 cup Mount Gay Eclipse Rum

4-6 cups chicken/vegetable stock

1/2 cup heavy cream

1/2 tsp ground nutmeg

garnish with chopped parsley and chives

## Method

Using 1/2 the butter, sauté garlic and ginger in oil mix. Add in onion, stir and sweat. Add potato, the rest of the butter and cook covered for 15 mins before adding pumpkin and stirring so it doesn't stick. When pumpkin starts to glaze and shine, add Mount Gay Eclipse Rum and allow liquid to reduce and almost evaporate. Cover vegetables with stock, reserving some to add later. Simmer till vegetables are soft, 25-30 mins. Strain, blend in small batches and re-strain pulp into liquid, adding more stock as wished. Add cream and ground nutmeg as you reheat and season to taste.

# Curried Carrot Soup
## with coriander pesto oil

*You Need*

*1/2 cup chopped onions*

*1 tbsp minced garlic*

*1/2 cup chopped sweet potato*

*3 cups chopped unpeeled carrots*

*1/3 cup oil mix*

*1 tbsp curry powder/paste*

*2 tbsp brown sugar*

*1/2 cup fresh coriander chopped*

*lime juice – to taste*

*1/2 cup Mount Gay Eclipse Rum*

*4-6 cups vegetable stock*

### Method

Sweat onions and garlic, sweet potato and carrots in oil mix. Add in curry powder, sugar, coriander, lime juice and Mount Gay Eclipse Rum, stirring in the flavour before pouring in stock. Simmer till vegetables are soft, 25-30 mins. Strain, blend in small batches, and re-strain pulp into original liquid. Reheat and season to taste. Garnish with coriander pesto oil.

### Coriander Pesto Oil

Blend 1/3 cup coriander, 1/4 tsp salt and pepper, 1 tsp lime juice and lastly, 1/2 cup oil until it's not only a fine, but also liquid consistency (to pour or spoon).

# Leek and Potato Soup
## with rum soaked apple bombs

### You Need

*4 cups chopped leek whites*

*1/2 cup chopped onion*

*1 stalk celery sliced*

*1 tsp minced garlic*

*1/2 cup oil mix*

*4 medium potatoes chopped*

*4-6 cups chicken/vegetable stock*

*1 cup heavy cream*

*1/2 tbsp butter*

*Apple Bombs*

*2-3 apples peeled, quartered and cored*

*1/2 cup Mount Gay Eclipse Rum*

### Method

Sauté all vegetables except potatoes in oil mix till onions and leeks are soft not brown. Add potato, then stock and simmer until soft to the fork. Strain, blend in small batches and re-strain pulp into liquid. Add cream and butter while reheating and season to taste with salt and pepper.

### Apple Bombs

You should get at least 4-5 1/2 tsp size bombs from each apple. Using a melon baller scoop bombs from the apples and soak in Mount Gay Eclipse Rum for 1 hr before serving.

# Shell Fish Rum Bisque

**You Need**

1-2 lb shrimp shells

1-2 lb lobster shells

1/2 cup oil mix

1/2 cup chopped onions

2 garlic cloves minced

1 whole scotch bonnet pepper

3/4 cup chopped carrots

1/2 cup chopped celery

2 tbsp butter

1 bay leaf

1/2 cup Mount Gay Eclipse Rum

2 tbsp tomato paste

1/3 cup flour

4-6 cups fish stock

heavy cream

## Method

Drizzle shells with a little oil mix, then roast in hot oven till pink or bright red. In a pot heat vegetables in oil and butter, add shells, bay leaf, rum, tomato paste, flour and stock. Simmer for 30 or 40 mins, skimming the surface occasionally. Strain and blend, the shells too if your machine can take it, adding in liquid to help lubricate. Re-strain into pot, season with salt and pepper and serve warm with a dash of Mount Gay Eclipse Rum and a splash of cream.

# Baked Rum Omelette

*You Need*

*a pan without plastic handles*

*1 tbsp butter*

*1 tomato chopped*

*1/3 cup chopped onion*

*1 tbsp chopped sweet pepper*

*1 small scotch bonnet pepper diced*

*4 eggs*

*1 tsp salt and pepper*

*1/3 cup milk*

*1 tbsp Mount Gay Eclipse Rum*

*1/4 cup grated cheese*

## Method

Pre-heat oven to 350-375⁰F. Add butter to pan and sweat vegetables. Beat eggs, salt and pepper, milk and Mount Gay Eclipse Rum well and pour into pan, adding butter if necessary, spreading over the cheese as the sides start to brown. Place pan in oven for 5-8 mins until the centre is firm to touch and egg is fluffy.

# Seared Tuna Salad
## with papaya rum dressing

### You Need

*1 red onion diced*

*1 green mango peeled and julienned*

*2 apples sliced*

*2 seedless oranges sliced or segments*

*fresh lettuce*

*red and yellow sweet pepper julienned*

*1-1 1/2 lb fresh tuna loin trimmed and shaped*

*1 tsp cracked black pepper*

*1 tsp toasted sesame seeds*

*1 tsp ground coriander*

*1/2 tsp salt*

*Papaya Rum Dressing\**

*2 tbsp papaya fruit or pulp*

*2 tbsp Mount Gay Eclipse Rum*

*1 tsp lime juice*

*dash orange juice*

*1/3 cup oil mix*

*\* Blend the first 4 ingredients and slowly*
*add the oil*

### Method

While heating pan to sear tuna in, toss and assemble salad vegetables and fruit. Roll tuna in the dry mix and place in a hot pan with little or no oil or butter. Sear each side evenly, about 2 mins a side so you can see the line where the outer edge is cooked and creeps inward. Stop at your level of rawness and let rest before slicing. Tuna may be prepared an hour or two before you actually need it. Slice thinly and drizzle with dressing. Garnish with chopped herbs and lime.

# Vegetable Rice Paper Rolls
## with molasses rum dip

*You Need*

*15-20 rice paper rounds/skins dipped in luke-*
*warm water until soft and drained*
*(please one at a time)*

*rice vermicelli noodles cooked to directions on*
*the package and chopped*

*1 avocado peeled, seeded and julienned*

*1 green papaya julienned*

*3 carrots peeled and julienned*

*1 onion julienned*

*1 tbsp basil leaves*

*1 tbsp mint leaves*

*Molasses Rum Dip*

*2-3 tbsp molasses*

*1/4 cup Mount Gay Eclipse Rum*

*2 tbsp lime juice*

*1/2 cup pineapple or orange juice*

*1 tbsp chopped coriander*

*1/2 scotch bonnet pepper diced*

Method

Place noodles a little from edge of paper and then the strips of avocado and other ingredients with a sprinkling of herbs. Roll edges away from you and repeat with rest of ingredients. For dip, heat molasses, Mount Gay Eclipse Rum, lime juice and fruit juice until reduced and thick. Cool down and add coriander and pepper. Serve on the side.

# Golden Fried Stuffed Plantain

You Need

1/4 cup boneless pork

1/4 cup boneless chicken

1 tbsp chopped garlic

2 tbsp diced sweet pepper

1 tsp diced scotch bonnet pepper

1 tbsp parsley

1 tbsp basil

2 tbsp oil

3 fl oz Mount Gay Eclipse Rum

2-3 large ripe plantains peeled and halved
    crossways

oil for deep frying 3-4 inches deep

## Method

Mince all the stuffing ingredients together and sauté in oil with the rum until cooked. Let cool before stuffing plantain. Make the hole with a wooden spoon handle, slowly and carefully, and enlarge by rotating the spoon. With a piping bag or by hand, pump the mix into the centre and then deep fry until golden brown. Drain oil on paper towel, sprinkle with brown sugar and serve.

# Jerk Chicken and Avocado Salad

## You Need

*1-2 kg boneless chicken breast chunks*

*jerk seasoning*

*1/4 cup Mount Gay Eclipse Rum*

*1 tsp lime juice*

*2 ripe avocados cubed*

*1 red onion sliced*

*2 tomatoes cut into wedges*

*1 yellow and 1 red sweet pepper sliced*

*assorted lettuce leaves*

*Vinaigrette Dressing\**

*shredded raw beet*

*3 tbsp vinegar*

*1 tbsp lime juice*

*1/2 cup of oil*

*\* Blend the first 3 ingredients and slowly add
the oil until emulsified*

## Method

Marinate chicken in jerk seasoning, Mount Gay Eclipse Rum and lime juice. Bake at 350°F for 10-15mins. Assemble salad including cubed avocado and serve with vinaigrette dressing.

# Steamed Seafood
## Lemongrass Saté

*1/2 lb shrimp*

*1/2 lb fish*

*1/2 cup chopped onion*

*1 tbsp chopped garlic*

*1/2 cup coriander and parsley leaves*

*2 tbsp Mount Gay Eclipse Rum*

*8-12 lemongrass stalks (6 inches in length)*

*Dip*

*3/4 cup fish stock*

*1/4 cup Mount Gay Eclipse Rum*

*1 tsp lime juice*

*1/2 tsp minced ginger*

## Method

In a food processor blend seafood, onions, garlic, herbs and Mount Gay Eclipse Rum until minced. Shape around lemongrass and steam for 5-8 mins until firm. For dip bring ingredients to a boil. Simmer for 20 mins then cool.

# Jazzy Mango Wings

*You Need*

*10–12 chicken wings*

*jerk seasoning*

*fresh mango or pulp*

*1/2 cup Mount Gay Eclipse Rum*

## Method

Marinate chicken in jerk seasoning, mango pulp,
Mount Gay Eclipse Rum, salt and pepper overnight. Pre-heat oven
to 350-375⁰F and bake for 25-30 mins.
Garnish with fresh herbs and mango slices.

# Curried Shrimp
## with cucumber pickle dip

**You Need**

1/2 cup chopped onion

1 tbsp curry powder/paste

1/4 cup fish stock

3/4 cup coconut milk

2 tbsp Mount Gay Eclipse Rum

1 lb cleaned shrimp

*Cucumber Pickle Dip*

2 cucumbers peeled and seeded

1 onion chopped

1 clove garlic minced

1 tbsp lime juice

3 tbsp vinegar

2 tbsp fresh parsley and thyme chopped

## Method

Sauté onion and curry powder in a little oil, then add the fish stock and simmer till reduced by half. Add coconut milk and Mount Gay Eclipse Rum till thickened. Quickly drop shrimp into boiling water until bright pink and toss into curry sauce. To make pickle, blend cucumber, onion, garlic, lime juice, vinegar and herbs. Season with salt and pepper.

# Spicy Grilled Shrimp
## with tamarind glaze

*You Need*

*bamboo skewers soaked in water for 30 mins*

*1lb peeled shrimp*

*1 tbsp jerk seasoning*

*1 tbsp minced ginger*

*1 tbsp lime juice*

*1 tbsp oil*

*Tamarind Glaze*

*3/4 cup tamarind syrup*

*1/2 cup Mount Gay Eclipse Rum*

*1/4 cup water*

Method

Marinate shrimp in remaining ingredients and skewer from head through to tail so shrimp is straight. Grill for 3-5 mins on each side, turning often as skewers burn quickly. Brush shrimp with glaze while cooking and before serving. To make glaze bring tamarind syrup, Mount Gay Eclipse Rum and water to a boil and simmer till thickened.

# Ceviche 151

1 sweet pepper

1 garlic clove

1/2 cup chopped onion

1/4 cup sliced red onion

1/4 cup diced cucumber peeled and seeded

1/4 cup chopped tomato seeded

1 tbsp chives

1 tbsp parsley

2 tbsp lime juice

1 tbsp oil

1/4 cup Mount Gay Extra Old Rum

1 lb fine cubed raw dolphin

1 lb fine cubed raw tuna

3/4 cup halved par-boiled shrimp

## Method

Roast sweet pepper and garlic clove for 20 mins in 400°F oven, peel skin and blend. Combine with remaining ingredients in a bowl and marinate fish for 10-15 mins before serving. Keep fish cold until use.

# Callaloo and Crab Dumplings
## in a pumpkin rum broth

### You Need

*2 cloves garlic minced*

*1/2 cup chopped onion*

*1/2 lb callaloo/spinach chopped*

*1 cup crab meat*

*1/2 cup fresh parsley and basil*

*1 tbsp lime juice*

*1/2 cup grated boiled potato*

### Pumpkin Rum Broth

*1 cup chopped pumpkin*

*2 tbsp brown sugar*

*1/4 cup Mount Gay Eclipse Rum*

*1 cup vegetable stock*

*2 tbsp butter*

### Method

Combine garlic, onion, callaloo, crab, herbs, lime juice and potato. Roll into golf ball size and steam in a colander over a pot of boiling water. For the broth cook pumpkin, sugar, Mount Gay Eclipse Rum in vegetable stock until pumpkin is soft. Blend, adding butter and a dash more Mount Gay Eclipse Rum.

# Ceviche 151

## You Need

*1 sweet pepper*

*1 garlic clove*

*1/2 cup chopped onion*

*1/4 cup sliced red onion*

*1/4 cup diced cucumber peeled and seeded*

*1/4 cup chopped tomato seeded*

*1 tbsp chives*

*1 tbsp parsley*

*2 tbsp lime juice*

*1 tbsp oil*

*1/4 cup Mount Gay Extra Old Rum*

*1 lb fine cubed raw dolphin*

*1 lb fine cubed raw tuna*

*3/4 cup halved par-boiled shrimp*

## Method

Roast sweet pepper and garlic clove for 20 mins in 400⁰F oven, peel skin and blend. Combine with remaining ingredients in a bowl and marinate fish for 10-15 mins before serving. Keep fish cold until use.

main
# events

# Roasted Duck Breast
## in a coconut curry sauce

### You Need

*4 duck breasts*

*1/2 cup chopped onion*

*1/2 cup pineapple chunks*

*2 tbsp curry powder/paste*

*3 cups chicken/vegetable stock*

*1/4 cup Mount Gay Eclipse Rum*

*1/4 cup pineapple juice*

*1 litre coconut milk*

*fresh basil and parsley to garnish*

### Method

Season duck breast with salt and pepper and sear skin side down until brown and crispy. Turn over and place in a 350-375°F oven for 10-12 mins. Let rest for 2-3 mins before slicing. For curry sauce cook onion, pineapple and curry powder in the mixed stock, rum and pineapple juice. Reduce and add coconut milk and cook for a further 15 mins until thick and sweet.

# Drunken Rum Punch
## Chicken Stew

### Method

Season chicken with salt and pepper and lime juice.
Sauté vegetables and chicken until chicken turns white, add juices,
sugar and Mount Gay Eclipse Rum
and stew for 1 1/2-2 hrs.

*You Need*

*1 whole chicken cut into pieces*

*1 tsp lime juice*

*3/4 cup chopped onion*

*2 garlic cloves chopped*

*1/2 tsp minced scotch bonnet pepper*

*1 litre pineapple juice*

*1 litre orange juice*

*1/4 cup brown sugar*

*1 cup Mount Gay Eclipse Rum*

*chives, parsley and tomato to garnish*

# Spicy Pork
## with orange rum glaze

*You Need*

*2 tenderloins trimmed of fat and skin membrane*

*1 tsp salt*

*1 tbsp black pepper crushed*

*1 tbsp all spice/pimento*

*a drizzle of oil for marinade*

*Orange Rum Glaze*

*1 litre orange juice*

*1 cup Mount Gay Eclipse Rum*

*1/4 cup honey*

*1/2 tbsp molasses*

Method

Season pork with spiced rub, sear all over in a hot pan and transfer to pre-heated 350°F oven for 15-18 mins or inside temperature of 160°F. Remove and let meat rest before slicing. For glaze combine ingredients in a pot, boil and simmer for 20 mins.

# Rack of Lamb
## with chocolate mint sauce

*2 tbsp oil*

*4-5 frenched (cleaned) lamb racks*

*1 tbsp salt and pepper*

*2 tbsp all spice ground*

*1 cup herbed breadcrumbs*

*Chocolate Mint Sauce*

*1 1/2 cups beef stock – demi glazed*

*1 tbsp brown sugar*

*1 tbsp lime juice*

*2 tbsp grated bitter sweet chocolate*

*3 tbsp Mount Gay Eclipse Rum*

*1/2 cup fresh mint leaves chopped*

### Method

Drizzle oil over lamb and season with salt, pepper and all spice. Coat each rack with breadcrumb mix. Roast in 350°F oven for 8-10 mins. Let rest for 2-3 mins before slicing. For chocolate sauce bring beef stock, sugar and lime juice to a boil. Reduce and remove from heat stirring in chocolate, Mount Gay Eclipse Rum and mint leaves just before serving.

# Grilled Steak
## with coffee-rum barbecue glaze

1 tbsp pimento

1/4 cup olive oil

1 tbsp salt and pepper

3/4 cup Mount Gay Eclipse Rum

1/2 cup onion and garlic puréed in a
   food processor

4-6 steaks (8-10 oz each)

*Barbecue Glaze*

2 cups tomato blended

1 cup very strong coffee

1/3 cup brown sugar

2 tbsp molasses

2 tbsp vinegar

2 cups Mount Gay Eclipse Rum

1/4 cup worcestershire sauce

2 onions and 2 garlic cloves chopped

3-5 drops of liquid smoke

### Method

Combine remaining ingredients and marinate steaks for 1 hr.
Grill steaks 5-8 mins per side basting with glaze and
let rest before serving.

### Barbecue Glaze

Bring ingredients to boil and simmer for
20-25 mins, stirring as it thickens.
Allow to cool before use.

# Calypso Steamed Mussels
## with vanilla rum and lime

### You Need

*1/3 cup chopped onion*

*2 garlic cloves chopped*

*2 lb mussels (or 10-15 per person)*

*4 tbsp butter*

*2 tbsp oil*

*12 fl oz / 1 bottle beer*

*1 tsp vanilla essence*

*1/4 cup Mount Gay Eclipse Rum*

*1/3 cup lime juice*

*1/2 cup chopped tomato*

*1/4 cup chopped parsley and basil*

### Method

Sauté onions, garlic and mussels in butter and oil mixture, stirring in beer, vanilla essence and finally Mount Gay Eclipse Rum, lime juice, tomato and herbs before serving. Season to finish with salt and pepper.

# Basil Dorado Baked in Phyllo

## with curry cream sauce

*You Need*

*1/2 cup basil leaves*

*2 tsp minced lemongrass*

*1 tsp minced scotch bonnet pepper*

*1/4 large onion*

*1 tsp salt and pepper*

*4-7 fish pieces (7-8 oz)*

*1 pack thawed phyllo pastry*

*1/2 cup melted butter*

*1 tbsp curry powder/paste*

*3 cups heavy cream*

*1/4 cup coconut milk*

*2 tbsp lime juice*

*1/4 cup Mount Gay Eclipse Rum*

*butter and flour roux to thicken*

Method

Make pesto by blending basil, lemongrass, pepper, half the onion, salt and pepper. Spread evenly on fish, season with salt and pepper and wrap each piece in phyllo about 3 sheets thick, buttered between each sheet and finally buttered over top before baking at 325-350°F for 6-8 mins, until corners are browning and fish feels firm to touch. In a pan, heat the remaining onion, chopped, mix in curry powder and then heavy cream and coconut milk, adding in lime juice and Mount Gay Eclipse Rum to taste when cream starts to rise. Whisk in small amount of roux till thickened. Remove from heat and pour over fish packets.

# Caribbean Lobster
## with rum-jerk butter

### You Need

a few 1-2 lb lobsters (or tails)
  halved and cleaned

1 tbsp melted butter

1/2 cup chopped onion

1 tbsp jerk seasoning

1/2 cup chopped sweet pepper

1/4 cup Mount Gay Eclipse Rum

2-3 tbsp butter

1/4 cup fresh lime juice

1/4 cup chives and parsley chopped

1/2 cup tomato concasse for garnish

### Method

Parboil the lobster until bright red, then put into a 300°F oven with a little melted butter. Sauté onion, jerk seasoning and sweet pepper in remaining melted butter and, removing from heat, pour in the rum and add butter stirring until it has melted evenly and creamily. Now add lime juice and herbs and serve over lobster or in dipping bowls on plate.

# Saffron <u>Sea Bass Steamed</u>
## in banana leaf

*You Need*

*banana leaves, washed and wiped clean*

*4 fillets sea bass*

*1 tsp saffron*

*1/2 cup Mount Gay Eclipse Rum and a tsp in*
*    each fish wrap*

*1/2 cup fresh coriander leaves*

*1 cup coconut milk*

*1/2 cup fish stock*

*2 tbsp lime juice*

### Method

Cut a square from the leaves and place a fillet in the centre of each topped with a sprinkle of saffron, Mount Gay Eclipse Rum, salt, pepper and coriander. Wrap package as close as possible, then steam in a colander over a pot of boiling water for 8-10 mins until fish is firm to touch. Heat coconut milk, fish stock and lime juice and reduce till thicker. Pour over opened plated packages.

# Stuffed Snapper
## in a ginger lime flambé

*You Need*

*4-5 snapper fillets*

*3/4 cup shrimp minced with onion and garlic*

*1/4 cup minced ginger*

*2 tbsp lime juice*

*3-4 1 inch butter cubes*

*1/2 cup Mount Gay Eclipse Rum*

*1/4 cup tomato concasse*

## Method

Slice fish diagonally, and stuff with shrimp mix.
Sear in butter, top down first, then flip over and place in
pre-heated 350°F oven for 5-8 mins until fish is firm to touch.
In a hot pan, place ginger and lime juice. Add butter cubes
one at a time and stir till well incorporated.
Add Mount Gay Eclipse Rum just before serving.
Lean the pan into the fire and pour mixture over fish.
Garnish with concasse and fresh herbs.

# Saffron Sea Bass Steamed
## in banana leaf

*You Need*

*banana leaves, washed and wiped clean*

*4 fillets sea bass*

*1 tsp saffron*

*1/2 cup Mount Gay Eclipse Rum and a tsp in*
  *each fish wrap*

*1/2 cup fresh coriander leaves*

*1 cup coconut milk*

*1/2 cup fish stock*

*2 tbsp lime juice*

## Method

Cut a square from the leaves and place a fillet in the centre of each topped with a sprinkle of saffron, Mount Gay Eclipse Rum, salt, pepper and coriander. Wrap package as close as possible, then steam in a colander over a pot of boiling water for 8-10 mins until fish is firm to touch. Heat coconut milk, fish stock and lime juice and reduce till thicker. Pour over opened plated packages.

# Pan Seared Scallop Crostini
## with herbed oil

*You Need*

*2 lb scallops*

*3 tbsp Mount Gay Eclipse Rum*

*2 tbsp oil*

*1/4 cup fresh lime juice*

*french baguette bread sliced diagonally and grilled*

*1/2 cup basil leaves blended with 1 cup oil, salt,*

*   pepper and 2 garlic cloves*

*1/2 cup chopped onion and garlic*

*1/4 cup tomato concasse*

Method

Marinate scallops in Mount Gay Eclipse Rum, salt and pepper, oil and lime juice for no longer than 5 mins. Sear in a hot pan for 2-3 mins each side or until golden brown. Only do 6-8 at a time so none break apart and all cook evenly. Serve with grilled bread crostini and spoon oil blend over scallops. Garnish with the chopped onion and garlic and the tomato concasse.

not so traditional

# side dishes

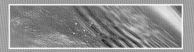

# Apple and Onion Tartlets

*You Need*

*1 cup peeled and sliced apples*

*3/4 cup sliced onions*

*1 tbsp brown sugar*

*zest of 1 orange*

*2 tbsp Mount Gay Eclipse Rum*

*juice from 2-3 limes*

*1 pack thawed phyllo pastry*

*1/2 cup melted butter*

Method

Sauté apples and onions in butter with sugar, orange zest, Mount Gay Eclipse Rum and lime juice and keep tossing until glazed and thick. Strain out extra liquid. Make phyllo cups with 3-4 buttered sheets, forming into shape with a muffin/cupcake baking pan. Fill with apple mixture. Pre-heat oven to 300ºF and bake until sides brown and the mix is bubbling. Sprinkle with sugar before serving.

# Grilled Vegetable Platter

*You Need*

*4-5 sweet peppers seeded and halved*

*3 onions sliced into rings*

*3/4 cup mushrooms*

*3 tomatoes quartered*

*1/2 lb sliced pumpkin*

*3/4 lb asparagus stalks*

*1/2 cup oil*

*1/4 cup balsamic vinegar*

*3 tbsp Mount Gay Eclipse Rum*

Method
Marinate vegetables in mixture of oil, vinegar, salt, pepper and rum.
Toss frequently then grill off in batches.
Can be served immediately or allowed to cool first.

# Warm Spinach and Sweet Potato Salad

## You Need

*2 onions sliced*

*1/4 cup sliced sweet pepper*

*2 cups spinach*

*3 tbsp oil*

*1 cup cubed sweet potato boiled*

*1/2 cup carrots roasted*

*2 tbsp butter*

*2 tomatoes chopped*

*1/4 cup chopped fresh herbs*

*1/4 cup Mount Gay Eclipse Rum*

## Method

Toss onions, peppers and spinach in hot oil.
Add sweet potato and carrots, then the butter, salt and pepper,
tomato, fresh herbs and rum. Serve warm.

# Mashed Sweet Potato
## with onions and crispy bacon

*You Need*

*2-3 cups peeled and chopped*
  *sweet potato boiled*

*1/4 cup heavy cream warmed*

*2 cloves garlic roasted*

*1/2 cup sliced onion and sweet pepper sautéed*

*2 tbsp butter*

*2 tbsp Mount Gay Eclipse Rum*

*1 pack bacon crisped on baking sheet in oven*

Method

In a mixer with a paddle, while the potato is still warm, mix in
the hot cream, garlic, onion and sweet pepper with the butter
and Mount Gay Eclipse Rum. Season with salt and pepper
and garnish with bacon and some fresh herbs.

# Coconut Rice and Peas

You Need

1/4 cup oil

2 garlic cloves chopped

2 onions chopped

1/2 scotch bonnet pepper chopped

1 sprig fresh thyme

2 lb rice

1/3 cup kidney beans
   soaked overnight in water

4 cups vegetable stock

1 1/2 cups coconut milk

1/4 cup Mount Gay Eclipse Rum

## Method

Heat oil in large pot and fry garlic, onions, pepper and thyme until the onions are translucent. Add rice and drained kidney beans and stir until well combined. Add stock to cover the rice by about 1 inch and then add coconut milk, and rum. Simmer for 40-50 mins until liquid has evaporated and rice is fluffed. Let rest/steam covered for 15 mins more before seasoning and serving. If you wish to use a squash, hollow out, removing seeds and drizzle with oil, salt and pepper. Bake at 350$^0$F in the oven for 30-35 mins. You can reheat rice-stuffed squash as a side or meal in itself.

# Spicy Island Slaw

1 cup grated carrot

1 cup grated cabbage

1/2 cup grated red cabbage

2 onions grated

1 red sweet pepper julienned

1 yellow sweet pepper julienned

1 tbsp minced ginger

*Dressing*

1/4 cup Mount Gay Eclipse Rum

1 cup vinegar

1/3 cup brown sugar

1 garlic clove minced

1 whole clove

## Method

Bring rum, vinegar, sugar, garlic and clove mix to a boil, melting the sugar. Add to the vegetables, mixing it well. Let stand for 15-20 mins and drain before serving.

# Roasted Beetroot and Pumpkin Salad

## You Need

*You Need*

*6 medium beets*

*2 lb pumpkin cut into 3/4 inch cubes*

*3 tbsp Mount Gay Eclipse Rum*

*1/2 cup fresh bean sprouts*

## Method

Pre-heat oven to 400°F. Wrap beets in foil with a little oil, salt and pepper and roast until beets are tender. In a pan, toss pumpkin with oil, salt and pepper, and the rum and roast for 25-30 mins. Remove skin from beets, quarter and serve hot or cold with fresh bean sprouts.

# sweet endings

# Baked Spicy Pumpkin
## and rum cheesecake

### You Need

13 oz cream cheese

2 oz sour cream

6 oz sugar

3 eggs

8 oz pumpkin steamed till soft to fork

3 oz melted white chocolate

pinch of saffron

2 tbsp Mount Gay Eclipse Rum

### Crust

6 oz finely ground cookies or biscuits

1 tbsp heaped sugar

2 oz butter

1/2 nutmeg grated

### Method

Blend cheese, sour cream and sugar until well mixed, add eggs one at a time and then pumpkin, chocolate, saffron and Mount Gay Eclipse Rum. Pour batter into cooled crust and bake at 350°F for 25-30 mins or until centre is firm to touch. Allow to cool and refrigerate before serving.

### Crust

Blend ingredients well, press down into buttered cheesecake pan (bottom drops out) and bake at 350°F for 10-15 mins until golden brown. Remove and cool.

# Coconut Rum Brûlée

## You Need

*1 cup milk*

*2 cups heavy cream*

*1 tsp vanilla essence*

*3 tbsp coc lopez or sweetened pina colada mix*

*5 egg yolks*

*3 tbsp Mount Gay Eclipse Rum*

*sugar (plus 1 tbsp added to coconut mix*
*    if not sweet enough)*

## Method

Heat milk, cream, vanilla and coconut mix until mixture starts to rise, remove from heat and whisk in egg yolks one at a time. Add Mount Gay Eclipse Rum and strain into ramekins (ovenproof ceramic cups) sitting in a warm water bath (halfway up sides) in a 300°F oven for 20-30 mins. Test centre with hand. It should be just a little runny. Cool before refrigerating. Caramelize tops with sprinkled sugar and torch before serving.

# Rum Banana Flambé

*You Need*

*1 cup flour*

*1 tbsp sugar*

*1/4 tsp salt*

*1 tbsp cream*

*1 1/2 cups milk*

*1 tbsp Mount Gay Eclipse Rum*

*3 or 4 beaten eggs*

*Sauce*

*2/3 cup orange juice*

*1 tsp lime juice*

*1 tsp grated orange zest*

*1 tsp grated lime zest*

*2-3 bananas sliced*

*1/4 cup sugar*

*1/4 cup butter*

*1/3 cup Mount Gay Eclipse Rum*

## Method

### Crêpes

Mix dry ingredients, add cream, milk, Mount Gay Eclipse Rum and eggs. Beat until smooth. Let stand for 30 mins. Melt a little butter in pan and add 1 tbsp of batter making a thin coat on bottom of pan. Let brown, and then repeat on other side. It cooks very quickly. Make crêpes until batter is gone or you have enough. Batter keeps well in fridge.

### Sauce

Boil juices and zest till thickened, 5-8 mins. Add bananas, sugar and butter. Pour in Mount Gay Eclipse Rum last and set alight before filling crêpe.

# Passionfruit, Mango and Rum Granita

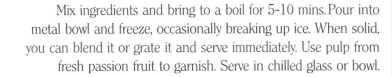

*You Need*

*1 cup mango pulp*

*1 cup passion fruit pulp*

*2 cups water*

*1 cup Mount Gay Eclipse Rum*

*1 cup simple syrup (1 lb sugar to*

   *2 cups water - boil)*

*2 tbsp lime juice*

Method

Mix ingredients and bring to a boil for 5-10 mins. Pour into metal bowl and freeze, occasionally breaking up ice. When solid, you can blend it or grate it and serve immediately. Use pulp from fresh passion fruit to garnish. Serve in chilled glass or bowl.

# Chocolate Coffee Sin Cake

*You Need*

*6 oz chopped chocolate*

*6 tbsp butter*

*3 tbsp brewed coffee*

*2 tbsp Mount Gay Eclipse Rum*

*1/2 cup ground almonds*

*1/2 cup sugar*

*4 eggs separated*

*shaved chocolate for garnish*

## Method

Pre-heat oven to 300⁰F. Melt (in a bowl over pan of simmering water) chocolate, butter, coffee and Mount Gay Eclipse Rum. Remove from heat and stir in almonds, sugar and yolks, one at a time. Whip egg whites until peaks form and fold in slowly to chocolate base. Pour mix into a greased 9 inch pan and bake for 40-45 mins or until tooth pick comes out clean. Let cool completely. Whip 1 cup heavy cream with 1 tbsp sugar and 3 tbsp Mount Gay Eclipse Rum until stiff and serve as a side topping.

# Deep Fried Ice Cream

## with toffee rum sauce

*You Need*

*1 cup cornflakes crushed*

*1/4 cup brown sugar*

*1 tbsp ground cinnamon*

*frozen ice cream, formed into small scooped balls*

*1/2 can Tate and Lyle golden syrup*

*1/2 cup heavy cream*

*1/4 cup Mount Gay Eclipse Rum*

## Method

Mix the cornflakes, brown sugar and cinnamon. Roll ice cream in cornflake mix and refreeze. Ice cream must be as cold and hard as possible. Boil golden syrup, cream and Mount Gay Eclipse Rum till cream rises, then remove and cool in a pot. Heat clean oil to deep fry ice cream balls, very hot, very quickly and serve right away with syrup.

# Rum Babas - Rum Soaked Bread Rolls

## You Need

*You Need*

*5 oz flour*

*1/4 tsp salt*

*2 tsp sugar*

*2 eggs*

*1 tbsp Mount Gay Eclipse Rum*
*and water mixed*

*1 tsp yeast*

*3 oz butter*

*Rum Mixture*

*1 cup Mount Gay Eclipse Rum*

*2 cups simple syrup (see p.110)*

*zest of 1 orange*

*2 whole cloves*

## Method

Mix flour, salt and sugar. In a bowl, mix egg, Mount Gay Eclipse Rum, and yeast. Add this to dry mix and cover to let rest and rise in a warm kitchen area. Grease a baking tray with the butter then, using two spoons, roll out small balls and lay on greased tray before baking at 200⁰F for 20-25 mins. Let rolls dry uncovered for up to 1 week before soaking in Mount Gay Eclipse Rum mixture.

# Chocolate Rum Soufflé

*5 oz bitter sweet chocolate chopped and melted*

*1 tbsp Mount Gay Eclipse Rum*

*3 egg yolks at room temperature*

*6 egg whites*

*1/3 cup sugar*

## Method

Mix chocolate, Mount Gay Eclipse Rum and yolks in a bowl. Butter and sugar sprinkle a 6-8 inch soufflé dish and pre-heat oven to 375⁰F. With a whisk, beat whites until soft peaks appear, add in sugar slowly while whipping, stir in half to chocolate mix and then fold the rest in gently. Pour into dish and run thumb around edge of top to help soufflé rise evenly. Bake until puffed, but soft in middle (jiggles), about 20-25 mins. Serve right away.

# About the Author

## paul yellin

**1971** born in New York City
**1973** moved to, raised and educated in Barbados, W.I.
**1993** began to cook professionally and has since
worked at and helped open successful and well
known restaurants in New York, Barbados, Toronto and Berlin.
**1996** launched "Edible Adventures" a full service catering company
whose clientele includes . . . '97 Pavarotti concert for Holders Opera
Season, Mount Gay / Remy Corporate Catering, The Australian
Consulate, The Italian Consulate, Film and Photo Shoot on-site
catering and baseball legend Ernie Bank's wedding
**2001** Won 1st place at Jamaica Spice Food Festival

My experience in restaurants and private catering
has now evolved into consulting. Opening new ventures is a
great chance to escape the repetition of a singular kitchen and
menu. I would like to thank the two men who most shaped my
career - and may not have realized they were...
Chef Larry Rogers and Master Chef Hans Schweitzer.

# About the Cocktails
## chesterfield browne

In 1994 Chesterfield Browne joined Mount Gay Distilleries Ltd
as the bartender at the Mount Gay Rum Visitors' Centre.
He has created many a recipe that has left a lasting impression
with his guests. He also created his own rum punch that has
become known as the best tasting rum punch in Barbados.

In 1997 he was nominated in the Barbados Minister of Tourism
Awards and won the coveted title of Bartender of the Year.
This outstanding achievement was accomplished again in 1998,
making him the only bartender in Barbados to have ever won
bartender of the year on two occasions. He was promoted to
International Brand Spokesperson in 1999 and travelled
throughout the world promoting the world's oldest and finest
rum - **Mount Gay Rum**.

Today, Chester is the Local Brand Specialist for Mount Gay
Distilleries' premium offer, Mount Gay Extra Old Rum.
He continues to represent the passion and pride of the people
who work at Mount Gay Distilleries and adds a
personal touch par excellence!

# Index